SPIRITUAL RENEWAL

D. JAMES KENNEDY

A Division of G/L Publications
Glendale, California, U.S.A.

© Copyright 1973 by D. James Kennedy
All rights reserved.
Printed in U.S.A.

Published by
Regal Books Division, G/L Publications
Glendale, California 91209, U.S.A.

Library of Congress Catalog Card No. 73-85947
ISBN 0-8307-0231-8

Chapters 4 and 5 of this book are based on material in *The
God of Great Surprises* (Chapters 1 and 11) by D. James
Kennedy. Published by Tyndale House. © Copyright 1973. Used
by permission.

CONTENTS

Dedicated to my wife Anne
who has faithfully supported
my ministry through these years.

GOD TALKS WITH ME

God Speaks
to Me Through
His Word

1

Over fifty years ago a young lawyer named Frank Morison set out to prove once and for all that the resurrection of Jesus Christ did not happen and that a careful study by a keen mind would reveal this immediately. He began to sort out truth from falsehood, to weigh and compare testimonies, to gather information for the writing of his book. He went through Scripture with a fine-tooth comb, not believing but purposely looking for errors, for contradictions, for corroboration to back up his thesis.

After many months of intensive study and investigation, Morison wrote his book. It is called *Who Moved the Stone?*, and it is one of the greatest books ever written to prove that the resurrection of Jesus Christ actually took place. Frank Morison became a believing disciple of the Nazarene as he studied the Scriptures to prove them false.

The same thing happened to Sir William Ramsey as he attempted to prove that the travels of Paul and his missionary journeys in the book of Acts were fictitious. Instead, he substantiated the book of Acts—and the rest of the Bible—as no other archaeologist had ever done.

The same thing happened to a German archaeologist, Adolph Deissmann, who went to the Holy Land in an attempt to destroy the Christian faith and its center. But in the process of doing so, he became a believer and wrote one of the most amazing books of evidence concerning the Bible. Again, the same thing happened to General Lew Wallace, who set out to disprove the deity of Jesus Christ and ended up writing the immortal *Ben Hur,* a novel which presents Jesus Christ as the living Son of God.

Since its writing, men have tried to disprove the Bible, to tear it apart, to destroy what is the very center of the Christian faith, the basis upon which all belief in Jesus Christ is founded. And they have all failed. God's Word has withstood the test of time and the onslaught of skeptical men. In fact, God seems to delight in taking the most devout skeptic and putting the idea into his head to disprove Scripture so that that man instead comes to be saved. The Bible cannot be destroyed by man any more than scooping water out of the ocean with a teaspoon will empty it.

We live in an age in which the Scriptures are ridiculed by some, ignored by others, and outrightly denied by most. But the overwhelming majority of people who treat the Bible lightly or deny its truths do not have the slightest idea of what it really teaches. To those who have come to it with an open mind and a searching heart, it has never failed them. And God has promised that it never will! His Word is as true and faithful as He Himself is.

The Bible *is* the core of Christianity, for from its pages come the doctrines and events that have shaped and directed the Christian faith. And God's Word teaches us about itself. As the Bible is our authority on Christianity and on man's personal relationship to Jesus Christ, we must understand the claims it makes and know why it has such authority and power.

God's Word Is Inspired

First of all, the Bible teaches that "all Scripture is given by inspiration of God, and is profitable for doctrine, for reproof, for correction, for instruction in righteousness: That the man of God may be perfect, thoroughly furnished unto all good works" (2 Tim. 3:16,17). This verse gives us the basic teachings of the Bible concerning itself.

Plenary Inspiration

"All Scripture. . . ." The word "all" is important, for here the Bible claims that "all Scripture," the totality of Scripture, is inspired by God; not just a part of it, but all of it. This is called plenary inspiration, meaning complete or full inspiration.

Plenary inspiration does not allow one to exclude, cafeteria-style, those particular parts of the Bible that do not suit one's tastes or opinions. Such inspiration includes the creation account in Genesis, the miracles of the Gospels, the virgin birth, Noah and the flood, and even Jonah and his great fish.

4

I mention these as some of the portions which skeptics and unbelievers are most likely to attack and deny. But the Bible does not make any exceptions when it says that "all Scripture is . . . of God."

"Is given by inspiration. . . ." The word "inspiration" comes from the Greek word *theopneustos* which means literally "God breathed." There are many people who say, "Oh, I believe the Bible is inspired, but so are the works of Shakespeare, Milton and other great writers." What they really mean is that these other works are inspiring, for there is a vast difference between something being inspired by God and being inspiring to man.

All Scripture is "God breathed." It is the very breath of God. No other writing or writer can make the claim of being "god breathed," and be substantiated in that claim.

When you come to the genealogical tables of the book of Numbers or the long series of "begats" in Matthew and Luke, you may be completely uninspired as you read them. You may find these tables totally lacking in anything which causes your heart to beat a little faster, but they are still God-breathed. The person who is discerning and has some knowledge of biblical tools can find precious jewels even in these chapters. The problem is not in the Scriptures, but in us, if we do not find them inspiring!

There is another fact you should remember concerning the inspiration of Scripture. It is the Scriptures which the Bible teaches are inspired. It is the writings that are inspired, not the writers—the apostles, the prophets, the men whom God used to put down His words.

This is far different from Mozart waking up in the morning with a melody running through his mind and rushing to set it down on paper. He was inspired. But in the case of the Bible, it is the Scripture which is inspired or, more accurately, expired—breathed out by God. This is the Bible's claim.

Verbal Inspiration

"Is given by inspiration. . . ." The inspiration of Scriputre is not only plenary, but also verbal. This means that not only the ideas but the very words of Scripture are inspired or God-breathed. God just did not give some men great thoughts and then leave to their imaginations how they were to write them down.

The Bible says, "I have put my words in thy mouth" (Jer. 1:9); "The word of the Lord hath come unto me" (Jer. 25:3). Over and over again we see the statement made that it is the words which are given by God and not merely the ideas. Thus we see that Scripture claims its inspiration is not only plenary, but verbal.

God's Word Is True

"Of God. . . ." Because the Scriptures are inspired by God, authored by God, they are infallible. This means they are incapable of error—without mistake. Whether or not the Scriptures are inspired is not the same question as whether or not the Scriptures are true. Though they are related, truth and inspiration are two different questions.

There are books written today which contain truths that are not inspired. It is conceivable that there may be some book written today which is entirely true, but which is still not inspired by God. Two and two are four. That's true, but not inspired.

If the Bible is inspired by God, then it will be true. If it is true in things that could not be known by any human process, then this would lead us to realize that it is inspired.

Neo-orthodox theologians of today speak of the Bible as being inspired without being true. But this is unthinkable. If something has been completely inspired by the God of all truth, the God who cannot lie, the God who knows all things, the God who is omniscient, then the Bible—His Word—must be true.

All of the statements of the Bible, all of its promises, all of its prophecies, all of its declarations are true because they are inspired by the God of truth. "They word is truth" (John 17:17), says Christ to His Father. Further, Jesus says, "The Scripture cannot be broken" (John 10:35). The Scriptures, therefore are infallible; they are true in all their parts. The totality of the Scriptures—not only the ideas, but the very words which contain them—are infallible, because they are inspired.

Over two thousand times the Bible claims Scripture to be inspired by God. "Thus saith the Lord" (Exod. 4:22); "The word of the Lord came unto the prophet" (2 Sam. 24:11); "The word of the Lord came unto me, saying" (Zech. 4:8); "Hear ye the word of the Lord" (2 Kings 7:1). From Genesis to Revelation, the Scriptures claim that the Bible is the Word of the living God revealed to man.

7

Prophecy and Fulfillment

The Bible verifies its claim of inspiration and even tells us how it will do so. God tells us one way to find out—through prophecy. He declares, "I am God, and there is none like me, declaring the end from the beginning, and from ancient times the things that are not yet done" (Isaiah 46:9,10). "Behold, the former things are come to pass, and new things do I declare: before they spring forth I tell you of them" (Isaiah 42:9).

The prophecies of God are not prophecies given in some vague and indeterminable fashion, so that fulfillment can be claimed no matter how things come out. Rather, the Bible contains hundreds upon hundreds of exact and unfailing prophecies. The prophecies of Scripture on so many issues are so plain, so detailed and specific, that any clear-thinking person can know whether or not a certain prophecy has come to pass.

The Test of Prophecy

God tells us "Despise not prophesyings" (1 Thess. 5:20). His next words are "Prove all things" (1 Thess. 5:21). But how do we prove prophecy? What is the test of prophecy?

God gives us the test of prophecy in these words, "When the word of the prophet shall come to pass, then shall the prophet be known, that the Lord hath truly sent him" (Jer. 28:9).

This does not mean a few isolated prophecies, occasional or accidental guesses, which are partly right and partly wrong. Anybody can guess, even guess right part of the time. It means there are vast

8

numbers of prophecies which will come to pass infallibly. This is the test: infallible fulfillment!

Prophecies of Christ

There are 333 Old Testament prophecies which concern the Person who is the very center of the teaching of the Bible, the main personage about whom the Scriptures were written, the central figure of our faith. That Person, of course, is Jesus of Nazareth, the Messiah of God, the Saviour of the world. Here the amazing wisdom of God is seen in all its glory.

The Old and New Testaments are divided by over 400 years of history. The Old Testament was written between 1400 B.C. and 400 B.C. approximately. It was then translated into a Greek language version called the Septuagint which was completed about 150 B.C. There can be no possible doubt that the Old Testament Hebrew Scriptures were completed hundreds of years before Christ was born. The New Testament which claims Jesus Christ to be the Messiah prophesied in the Old Testament was written during the first century A.D.

One of the great functions of the Old Testament was to promise that the Messiah was to come in the fulness of time to redeem mankind. But how could this Messiah be identified? The identification would be done in this way: various aspects of His life would be prophesied, thus forming a picture of the Messiah. The prophecies are like pieces of a jigsaw puzzle. In themselves the prophecies do not mean a great deal, but when put all together, they form a perfect picture of the Messiah by which He can be identified.

The Old Testament contains 333 prophecies concerning the coming of the Messiah alone, as well as hundreds of other prophecies about Him. No other book in the world even pretends to do such a thing as this. There is no other person in the world whose life has been so minutely described in all of its details long before He was born.

Can you imagine someone similarly prophesying the life of Abraham Lincoln? To equal the accuracy of the biblical prophecies concerning Christ, Lincoln's prophet would have had to describe not only the nation in which he was born but also the state and city. He would have had to describe his parents, his grandparents, his great-great-great-great-grandparents, and trace his lineage back through the centuries.

In addition, he would have had to describe the character he would have, the conduct he would exhibit, the life he would live, and the offices he would hold. He would have had to foretell even minute details of Lincoln's life and career.

He would also have had to know where the future president would live, where he would work, and even what his family and friends would think about him.

To top it all off, he would have had to foretell how Lincoln's life would end, not only that America's sixteenth president would be assassinated, but also that he would be shot in the head. At the same time, he would have to add approximately 320 other details of Lincoln's life and complete all his prophecies no later than A.D. 1350.

Some of the messianic prophecies of the Old Testament fulfilled in Jesus Christ are: He would come through the seed of a woman, not a man. He would be born of the lineage of Abraham, of the ancestry of Isaac, and of the line of Jacob.

He would come at a certain set time, would come to the second Temple (later destroyed in A.D. 70 as predicted by Christ), would come out of the tribe of Judah, and be descended from David. (No Jew today can prove that he is a direct descendant of David or that he is of the tribe of Judah, because all of the chronological tables were destroyed by Titus and Vespasian in A.D. 70).

Furthermore, the Bible described the very date on which Christ would be born—483 years after the decree went out from Artaxerxes, after the Babylonian captivity to rebuild the Temple. We are told in Scripture that Christ would be born of a virgin in the city of Bethlehem in the state of Judea. Great persons would come to adore Him.

He would be preceded by John the Baptist, would be anointed by the Holy Spirit, and would be a prophet like Moses. The Scriptures prophesied that He would enter into a public ministry, would begin it in Galilee, and would preach publicly in Jerusalem.

Of His character, the Old Testament tells us that He would be poor, meek, and lacking in ostentation. He would also be tender and compassionate and work miracles. He would be without guile. He would bear the reproach of those about Him, would be rejected by His own brothers, hated without cause, and finally rejected by the Jewish rulers.

Jews and Gentiles would band together to destroy Him. He would be betrayed by His own friend with whom He had eaten, and His disciples would forsake

Him. He would be betrayed and sold for thirty pieces of silver, and His price would be given for a potter's field. His enemies would spit upon Him, scourge Him, and nail Him to a cross.

The Scriptures are even more specific about His death. He would be forsaken by His friends and by God. He would be mocked by priests and given gall and vinegar to drink. His suffering would be intense, but it would also be vicarious. He would be silent in the midst of all His tortures. His garments would be torn off and lots cast for them. He would intercede for His murderers.

He would be numbered among transgressors, for His death would be among thieves. Not one of His bones would be broken, but His hands and feet would be pierced. He would be buried with the rich, but His flesh would not see corruption because He would arise from the dead, ascend into heaven, and sit at the right hand of God. And then His gospel would be preached even to the Gentiles.

Add to these some three hundred more prophecies and you have the life of Jesus Christ as pictured in the Old Testament; prophecies inspired by God, written down by man, and fulfilled by Christ. Each tiny piece of prophecy, when fitted together, gives us a perfect mosaic describing Jesus so intimately, so accurately, that those who have examined it cannot help but be impressed by it—and by Scripture.

Other Fulfilled Prophecies

The evidence of prophecies concerning the Messiah is overwhelming; surely anyone can recognize the fact that God's hand is in the writings of Scripture.

But there is another form of prophecy in the Bible which helps to convince even the most skeptical that Scripture is divinely inspired and written. These prophecies concern cities and nations which have existed upon the earth.

Prophecies of Tyre

The great commercial seaport city of Tyre was on the eastern end of the Mediterranean, not far west of Galilee. For two thousand years Tyre had grown in importance until it was the sea capital of the world, just as Babylon was the land capital. Into Tyre flowed the riches of Tarshish, the horses of Armenia, the gold and silver of Java, the ivory of Damascus, the linens of Egypt, and the learning of the Greeks. Tyre, the beautiful; Tyre, the great.

But in its prosperity the people of Tyre had turned their backs on God. They had despised His people, the Jews, and set themselves against them. And for their sins God declared their doom years before it actually occurred.

Through the prophet Ezekiel, God said of Tyre: "And they shall destroy the walls of Tyrus, and break down her towers: I will also scrape her dust from her, and make her like the top of a rock. It shall be a place for the spreading of nets in the midst of the sea: for I have spoken it, saith the Lord God. . . . and they shall lay thy stones and thy timber and thy dust in the midst of the water. . . . I will make thee like the top of a rock: thou shalt be built no more: for I the Lord have spoken it" (Ezek. 26:4,5,12,14).

After the Lord had spoken these words through the prophet Ezekiel, Nebuchadnezzar, the great king of Babylon, attacked Tyre. For thirteen years his army beat against the walls of Tyre, and for thirteen years the people inside the city withstood the onslaught. But finally the gates crumbled, and the horses of Nebuchadnezzar's army rode into the streets of Tyre. The blood of its people flowed in the streets as the towers were knocked down, the fortresses were overthrown, and the spoil was taken away. Nebuchadnezzar's army left the dust to settle upon the ruined heap of Tyre.

Skeptics might say that Ezekiel wrote down these events after they had taken place, predating the writings and them palming them off as prophecy. But many of the details of the prophecy remained unfulfilled, to be completed later—much later than Ezekiel's own lifetime.

God had said of Tyre that he would destroy the walls and break down the towers. He said that her stones and timbers and the dust of the city would be laid in the sea. Nebuchadnezzar's victory over Tyre had left the city desolate; not a citizen remained alive. Yet a hundred years after the defeat of Tyre, her broken walls still jutted into the sky, forming against the horizon an open declaration that the Word of God remained unfulfilled.

Another hundred years passed, and still the broken walls stood. The site of Tyre was still littered with the stones and timbers of ruined houses. And why not? Who would bother to take an empty city, level it to the ground and cast its very dust and rubble into the sea? So for fifty more years the ruins of Tyre remained.

But God had also said of Tyre: "Behold, I am

against thee, O Tyrus, and will cause many nations to come up against thee, as the sea causeth his waves to come up" (Ezek. 26:3). The ocean does not cast all its waves onto the shore at one time. Wave upon wave, they follow one another. Only the wave of Nebuchadnezzar had yet rolled over Tyre. Other waves were still to follow.

And so, in the year 333 B.C., 250 years after Nebuchadnezzar left Tyre in ruins, there appeared on the horizon to the north an august personage, Alexander the Great, wearing silver mail and a golden plumed helmet, riding astride a white horse. Behind him, a massed Greek phalanx marched. And before him, his fame cast terror throughout the whole of the Persian Empire.

On the plains of Issus, Alexander gave Persia's mighty King Darius III his first taste of defeat. Darius escaped, abandoning his camp and harem to the enemy. But Alexander did not pursue the fleeing king. Instead, he turned to the sea to seal off the seaports that supplied the Persian army.

When Alexander reached the site of old Tyre, he found nothing but ruins and rubble. But one-half mile out in the Mediterranean, glistening in the sun, lay new Tyre, rebuilt upon an island and surrounded by a 150-foot wall. New Tyre was determined never to suffer the fate of old Tyre.

Alexander recognized that this new fortified city was a threat to his security. It gave Persia control of the sea and supplied its army. He laid plans to storm the city.

Having determined his course of action, Alexander began building a causeway or mole—the first of its kind in the history of warfare—from the mainland to the island city half a mile away. Material was needed for the construction. And so the stones, the timber and the rubble of old Tyre were scraped up and cast into the sea. The remaining walls were broken down. Even the very dust of the city was scraped up from the rock and cast into the sea.

Employing his troops and the heartiest inhabitants of the area, Alexander literally leveled mainland Tyre to build his causeway. Almighty God used even Alexander the Great to fulfill His prophecy!

But the prophecy concerning Tyre was not yet entirely fufilled. For God had said of Tyre, "Thou shalt be built no more: for I the Lord have spoken it" (Ezek. 26:14). This is an incredible prophecy, for the Bible is full of cities that were destroyed and then rebuilt later on. Jerusalem and Rome were utterly destroyed, yet both were rebuilt. And this is true of hundreds of other cities.

Yet though some of the inhabitants of Tyre moved to an island offshore in the Mediterranean, mainland Tyre was obliterated and remains so today, just as God prophesied. The site of old Tyre is only a bleak beach with bare rocks shining in the sun, "a place to spread nets upon" (Ezek. 26:14).

Prophecies of Sidon

God also pronounced judgments upon the city of Sidon, thirty miles to the north of Tyre. God said, "Behold, I am against thee, O Zidon; . . . and they shall know that I am the Lord, when I shall have executed judgments in her, and shall be sanctified in her. For I will send into her pestilence, and blood into her streets; and the wounded shall be judged in the midst of her by the sword upon her on every side; and they shall know that I am the Lord" (Ezek. 28:22,23).

Around 345 or 344 B.C., Artaxerxes III attacked and destroyed Sidon. The city was set aflame, and blood flowed in the streets of Sidon as some forty thousand citizens perished in the holocaust. But God did not prophesy of Sidon, as He did of Tyre, that "thou shalt be built no more." So although old Tyre was a greater city than Sidon, it no longer exists, while a rebuilt Sidon remains today, a small town in Lebanon.

Prophecies of Ashkelon

In 600 B.C., the prophet Zephaniah pronounced the doom of God upon Ashkelon, declaring "Ashkelon a desolation" (Zeph. 2:4). Yet the city continued to grow and prosper. It became the hometown of Herod the Great, and in his lifetime he built a huge stadium and temple there. During the time of Christ, 600 years after the prophecy was given, Ashkelon was a great seat of learning. But then in A.D. 1270, General Baibars, the Sultan of Egypt, utterly demolished Ashkelon and left it abandoned. Ashkelon remained a desolation until the State of Israel was established in 1948 when it was again rebuilt and resettled.

Prophecies of Babylon

Perhaps the most amazing prophecies recorded in the Bible concern Babylon, one of the greatest cities in the history of the world. Already one of the more famous cities of antiquity, Babylon under King Nebuchadnezzar became the most important city in western Asia. Herodotus, the Greek historian, describes the walls of Babylon as being wide enough for four chariots to ride side by side along their tops. The city was laid out in a square, and its outer walls on each side, according to Herodotus, were fourteen miles on each side. The famed hanging gardens of this massive city, with terraces rising three hundred feet in the air, were an engineering and architectural triumph, so much so that they were known as one of the seven wonders of the world. The fame and size of Babylon were rivaled only by its beauty and wealth.

But what did God say about mighty Babylon? Chapter after chapter of the Old Testament is filled with minute details of what would happen to this great city. Here are some of the prophecies:

"And I will render unto Babylon and to all the inhabitants of Chaldea all their evil that they have done in Zion in your sight, saith the Lord. Behold, I am against thee, O destroying mountain, saith the Lord, which destroyest all the earth: and I will stretch out mine hand upon thee, and will roll thee down from the rocks. . . . And Babylon shall become heaps, a dwelling place for dragons, an astonishment and an hissing, without an inhabitant. . . . Though Babylon should mount up to heaven, and though she should fortify the height of her strength, yet from me shall spoilers come unto her, saith the Lord. . . . The broad walls of Babylon shall be utterly broken . . ." (Jer. 51:24,25,37,53,58).

Over and over again, God speaks not only of Babylon's destruction, but also of Babylon's desolation.

"Thou shalt be desolate for ever, saith the Lord. . . . the land of Babylon a desolation without an inhabitant. . . . none shall remain in it, neither man nor beast, but that it shall be desolate for ever" (Jer. 51:26,29,62).

"And Babylon, the glory of kingdoms, the beauty of the Chaldees' excellency, shall be as when God overthrew Sodom and Gomorrah. It shall never be inhabited, neither shall it be dwelt in from generation to generation: neither shall the shepherds make their fold there.

"But wild beasts of the desert shall lie there; and their houses shall be full of doleful creatures; and owls shall dwell there, and satyrs shall dance there. And the wild beasts of the islands shall cry in their desolate houses, and dragons in their pleasure palaces: and her time is near to come, and her days shall not be prolonged" (Isaiah 13:19-22).

Babylon's time was truly near to come! Hardly a generation had passed from the giving of Isaiah's prophecy till Sennacherib, King of Assyria, marched down from Nineveh and in 689 B.C. leveled Babylon to the ground. But Esar-haddon, Sennacherib's son, soon rebuilt Babylon on the same site during his short reign from 680-669 B.C.

During the sixth century B.C. Babylon waxed as Nineveh waned, until in 612 B.C. the Babylonians and Medes combined forces to raze Nineveh to the ground. For the next two thousand years even the very site of Nineveh was unknown to the civilized world. But Babylon continued to grow, and prosper until it reached the pinnacle of its fame, power and wealth during the reign of King Nebuchadnezzar from 605 to 562 B.C.

Had Isaiah prophesied wrongly? Nineveh was gone, but Babylon was greater than ever. But then early in Nebuchadnezzar's reign came the prophet Jeremiah, echoing the words of Isaiah as he too prophesied the destruction and desolation of Babylon.

About 556 B.C. Belshazzar, grandson of Nebuchadnezzar and son of Nabonidus, ascended the throne of Babylon as co-regent with his father. Combined forces of Medes and Persians laid siege to Babylon, breached the walls, imprisoned Nabonidus, killed Belshazzar and captured the city. Darius the Median then laid claim to Babylon, and its empire came to an end.

In 539 B.C. Cyrus the Great took Babylon without a struggle. The glory of Babylon was already gone, and finally about 484 or 486 B.C., Persia's Xerxes the Great captured Babylon and destroyed much of what little still remained. In 275 B.C. the remaining inhabitants of Babylon were removed to the newer city of Seleucia. First destroyed and then depopulated, Babylon had in truth become a desolation as prophesied. The end of the once-great city came just as God said it would.

To this day, Babylon remains desolate and uninhabited by any human being. Believing and fearing that "satyrs" or goat-headed demons prowl the deserted ruins, no Arab will stay overnight in Babylon. Only wild beasts of the desert live there now. "Babylon is fallen, is fallen" (Isaiah 21:9).

To an unbeliever who disbelieves that the Bible is the inspired, infallible Word of God, Babylon is a gauntlet thrown down by God Himself. For a simple way to disprove the Bible and to discredit its prophecies would be to rebuild Babylon. There once was a man who thought he was God and who tried to rebuild Babylon. He was Alexander the Great.

At the time, Alexander had already conquered most of the then known world, including Babylon. Following his conquest of much of Asia, Alexander returned to Babylon in 323 B.C. He planned to open and develop a sea route from Babylon to Egypt, as he had military designs on Arabia. To accomplish his goals, Alexander felt he would need a navy of at least a thousand ships. So he and his men set about building Babylon into a great naval base.

The work of excavating and rebuilding began, but then the hand of God fell upon Alexander. He was seized with a great fever and died within a few days in what was left of Nebuchadnezzar's palace. Babylon remained a desolation, just as God had declared it would be.

"I am God, and there is none like me, declaring the end from the beginning, and from ancient times the things that are not yet done" (Isaiah 46:9,10).

Fulfilled prophecy is a proof of the infallibility and authority of the Scriptures; it proves that this is not merely a book written by enlightened men but the Word of God which speaks all truth and knows all things.

God's Word and You

Once you come to grips with the reality of the truth of the Bible, once you begin to experience the power behind the words, great things begin to happen. The Word of God becomes real, alive and vibrant. No other book more rightly deserves your attention; no other book can make the time you spend in its study so rewarding and worthwhile.

Skeptics will continue to doubt that the Bible is the Word of God, that it is actually God speaking to man. They will continue to mock it and to jeer at its message.

But we have God's own promise that His Word is true and that it will outlast all else that exists on this earth. "Heaven and earth shall pass away, but my words shall not pass away" (Matt. 24:35).

God Speaks
to Me as I Study
His Word

2

We have seen something of the inspiration and authority of the Scripture. Now we will consider how to properly study the Word of God. Yes, there is a method of studying the Bible so that you grow as you read. This means more than just a random daily reading of the Bible determined by sticking your finger anywhere in the book and then spending two minutes reading the passage where you landed. To read and grow, you must learn how to study, how to apply yourself to this most unique book. Bible study is a science, and, like any other science, it takes some fundamentals to apply it.

We must always remember that the Bible is different from any other book in this world because it was written by inspiration of God. It is, in fact, the living, quickening, lifegiving breath of God Himself.

The Bible is more than a book; it is a whole library. It contains every treasure, every promise, every hope the Christian will have in this world. We are to study it. We are to meditate upon it. We are to hide its words in our hearts, to memorize it so that God can use it to transform our lives. It is out of a desire for God's Word that we read and feed—and grow. The Bible says, "As newborn babes, desire the sincere milk of the Word, that ye may grow thereby" (1 Pet. 2:2).

If you have already begun to study the Word of God, you probably began in the Gospel of John. This is a good place to begin. It will give you an overview of who Jesus was, what He did on earth, and what His death means for each human being. When you have finished reading John, go on to read the epistle to the Romans, the central epistle of the New Testament. In it, Paul gives us all the basic doctrines of Christianity. Don't be discouraged, however, if you have trouble understanding everything in Romans at the end of your first reading. Many men have made lifelong studies of this book, and each reading reveals new truths to them!

Study Daily

In studying the Scriptures, it is important to set aside a certain time each day, preferably in the morning, so that God can use it to bless your life as you begin the day. This is a better time, I feel, than at night after you have already managed to mess up the day. It is best to begin in the morning with His Word and with prayer. However, you may find that the evening offers more peace and quiet after the day's activities are behind you.

But whichever time you choose, stick to it. Everything in the world will happen to make you want to give up your study time "just this once." "I'm late for work, so Bible study will have to go." "I'm just too tired to apply myself tonight." "I just don't have time to study today."

If you are really serious about growing as a Christian through studying the Word of God, make up your mind not to let anything deter you. Once you develop a daily habit of Bible study, you will find it is not a chore, but rather something you look forward to and without which you feel incomplete.

Expectation

Remember, too, your attitude as you come to the Bible is all-important. You must come expectantly, believing in its truths and power for your life, and praying to God that the Holy Spirit will enlighten your mind to understand and receive the Word He has for you.

Don't forget that you are coming to the Word of the living God; to a God who delights to bless your life, who has something for you every day and who wants to speak to you. The Bible is God's way of speaking to you, just as prayer is your way of speaking to Him. So be prepared for great things to happen in your life and in your walk with the Lord through your Bible study—for they surely will happen!

Observation

As you study the Bible, develop the habit of observation, of really looking at what you read. When you read a portion of Scripture—whether it be a few verses, a chapter or an entire book—learn to really look at what you are reading. Then it will stick with you. Too often people read through a portion of Scripture and then get up and go away, hardly knowing what they have read.

So try to observe carefully. You will find it a helpful habit to keep a notebook indicating which portion of Scripture you have read and what you have observed in it.

The great naturalist, Louis Agassiz, used to stress that his students learn the art of observation. He gave one young man the assignment of observing everything he could about a frog. The student looked at the frog for about half an hour, wrote down everything he saw, and then came back to his teacher with the question, "What do I do now?"

"Look at it some more," replied Agassiz.

The young man went back for another hour, and the same command was repeated when he returned to his teacher. The whole day passed in this way, then another day, and another, and a fourth, until finally the student had discovered that there was a vast amount of information about the frog that he had not noticed at all previously.

So a notebook on what you are reading is most helpful. You may also wish to make notes in your Bible as you read. Every Christian should have at least one Bible that he can write in for reference. Then, the next time you read a passage, your previous notes will be there to help you.

As you go over and over the Scriptures, you are going over ground which is tremendously wealthy,

ground in which are buried many precious gems.
Read carefully and note what you read.

Interpretation

After you have observed as much as you can
about the text you have read, the next step is to in-
terpret what the Scripture is saying. There are some
basic hermeneutical (interpretive) principles that
you should understand and apply. The Bible is its
own interpreter. Difficult passages are often ex-
plained in context or in other places in Scripture. "A
text without a context is a pretext." Some people say
that the Bible can be made to say anything you want
it to say. This is true if you ignore the basic principles of hermeneutics of interpretation.

For example, the Bible says, "Then Judas . . .
went out and hanged himself," "go, and do thou
likewise," and "that thou doest, do quickly" (Matthew
27:3,5; Luke 10:37; John 13:27). Yes, the Bible
actually says all this! But it makes each statement in
three different places in three entirely different con-
texts about three completely different situations. The
Bible doesn't mean at all what these verses are saying
when wrongly combined in this way.

So we need to consider certain principles in our interpretation. First of all, ask yourself, "What does
the text really say?" Don't come to a false conclusion
as to what it says but look at the text very carefully.
For example, how many times have you heard, "The
Bible teaches that money is the root of all evil"?
Many people would swear that the Bible says this.
But what Scripture actually says is, "The love of
money is the root of all evil" (1 Timothy 6:10). Do

you see the vast difference in meaning between these two statements?

Immediate Context

The second principle to apply when observing Scripture is the immediate context in which the text is found. Seeing the jewel in its setting, where God has placed it, often helps us to better understand what the text really means.

Total Context

Thirdly, consider the text as a part of the total context of the Bible. Since the Bible explains itself, if somethng is obscure in one place, there will be other places where it speaks more clearly. Therefore you should learn to use a concordance so that you can look up different passages in the Bible.

A good commentary is an invaluable aid to the student of the Scripture. After you have interpreted a passage or verse as best you can, the commentary or commentaries will help you to better understand what you have read. You need to be careful, however, not to rely only on the commentary; use it after you have first interpreted the Scripture for yourself and then compare interpretations.

There are many good commentaries and some that are not so good. One of the best is *Matthew Henry's Commentary;* it has stood the test of time and is acclaimed as one of the best. But check around and discover other good commentaries for yourself by asking friends, pastors, or knowledgeable lay people. It is an investment which will pay off as the years go by.

Application

After you have observed and interpreted your Scripture reading, then comes the final step in Bible study, applying what you have read to your own daily life. We are not simply to read Scripture and then go our way forgetting it. We are to apply it to ourselves. What does this mean? It means that there are certain things you should be on the lookout for as you read—verses or sections you might want to underline, memorize, or read over and over again.

Promises

One thing you should look for is a promise from God. If there is something that God says He will do, underline it. (You might want to use a differenct colored pencil for underlining the promises of God, the commandments of God, etc. In this way you can keep them straight in your mind and spot them instantly when you open your Bible.) It is a good practice to learn as many of the promises of God as you can.

Many people do not live their Christian lives to the fullest because they are not aware of God's promises so that they can claim them for their own. These promises are like uncashed checks if you do not apply them to yourself; the cash is there if you do with the check what you are supposed to do, that is, cash it. It has been stated that a Christian's whole life at its conclusion will be seen to have been simply an unfolding of God's promises which He has made and the believer has claimed.

You have trusted Christ for your eternal salvation. Now you must learn to trust Him also in every aspect of your daily life. As you learn the promises He has made to you, it will become easier for you to trust Him for material things, for your family, for your business and social affairs, for your finances, in short, for every segment of your life.

Remember, God is concerned with the smallest detail of your life; even "the very hairs of your head are all numbered" (Matt. 10:30). So, learn to rest upon Him. Learn the secret of spiritual serenity; learn to rely upon the promises of God.

Commandments

Secondly, application of Scripture means being aware of commandments for you to obey. If you truly love Christ, you will want to keep His commandments. (See John 14:21.) Of course, in order to keep them you must know them. There are many commandments which Christians do not keep simply because they never realized these commandments were written down in Scripture. God's commandments apply to every area of your life and will greatly enrich your walk with the Lord as you learn them and obey them.

As you do so, you will realize that God is a wise and loving Father. His commandments are not burdensome, but are given by Him to make our lives as rich and full as possible. If you are a parent, you know that the commandments you give your children come out of a heart of love and are designed as best you know for their well-being. God, as our heavenly Father, commands us with both infinite love and total knowledge; therefore, fulness of life will come to you in the same measure that you obey His commandments.

Examples

Thirdly, there may be an example in Scripture for you to follow. The Scriptures are filled with examples, some good, some bad, but all are examples from which you can learn valuable lessons. There are many great, godly men and women whose examples will encourage and inspire you and help you to grow further in the Lord.

All of these things will help your daily time of Scripture reading, meditation and study to be a time of rich blessing and fulfillment in your life rather than a duty to perform. As you read the Word of God today and throughout the rest of your life, use these methods of observation, interpretation and application in your Bible study. As you do so, you will find they can mean the difference between an exercise that is boring, monotonous and dry, and a growth experience in the Lord that is a continuing and ever more exciting adventure with Him.

I TALK WITH GOD

How I
Speak to
God

3

We have considered the authority of the Scriptures and the importance of Bible study to learn better how God speaks to us. Now let us consider the other half of that dialogue: how we speak to God.

Men with empty water bottles stagger over burning desert sands. They die, and their bones bleach in the blazing sun, while nearby palm trees grow and flourish. But the hot winds that sift sand over their bleached bones only cause the green branches of those trees to flutter in the breeze, because the trees have roots which reach down and take hold of unseen fountains below.

So it is today in the deserts of our modern cities, where many perish and are consumed in the noontime heat and pressures of daily life. The anxieties of life—making a living, tensions of the office, the pressures of home and the difficulty of family life in a modern world—all contribute to wither the soul and bring many to the end of themselves and total ruin.

At the same time, however, in the same city deserts, others smile and seem to float through their problems on a river of serenity that causes onlookers to be utterly amazed. But if you look deep into those smiling eyes, you will see in their souls the luxuriant growth that comes only where roots have taken hold of hidden fountains beneath. They have found stability and peace of mind because their roots reach deep beneath the surface turmoil of everyday life to the fountain of communion with the living God. They overcome each day's trials and tribulations because they are firmly rooted in communion with the Water of Life who makes a living fountain to spring up in their souls. This communion with the Living God, the "fountain of life," is called prayer.

The Art of Prayer

Prayer is not only a universal instinct, it is also an art. As theology is the queen of the sciences, prayer is the noblest of the arts, surpassing music, painting and sculpture. The divine art of prayer is personal linkage with the Eternal. It is communion with power unseen which transforms lives in ways that are absolutely unaccountable when one looks at the desert winds which blow about our modern world.

Prayer is the most needed art in our time. It is also the most difficult art to learn. It is often said that "Satan trembles when he sees the weakest saint upon his knees." But he does more than tremble. He uses all of his wiles—and he has many—to keep us from prayer. He uses the pressure of the world, the crowding of the daily schedule and the tyranny of the urgent to keep us from the place of quiet communion with God.

When we are not in communion with God, our souls find no rest, no solitude, no peace. We are not strengthened because we do not wait before the Lord in prayer. We do not rise up with wings and fly because we do not kneel down in prayer and wait before Him.

We all need to learn the art of prayer. One of the greatest reasons for the rise of mental illness in the nation today is a lack of personal prayer. The Scripture says, "Be careful (or anxious) for nothing; but in every thing by prayer and supplication with thanksgiving let your requests be made known unto God. And the peace of God, which passeth all understanding, shall keep your hearts and minds through Christ Jesus" (Phil. 4:6,7).

If we are not in communion with the living God, if our requests with thanksgiving are not made, if our eyes are not fixed upon the Christ of perfect peace, then our hearts indeed will be filled with anxiety. They will be torn this way and that. And this is exactly what has driven so many people first into mental depressions and breakdowns and then into the asylums of our country. And there are countless others who never enter mental hospitals, yet they live joyless, anxiety-ridden lives without peace because they lack a relationship with God and have no personal communion with Him through prayer. How needful it is that we learn how to pray.

"Lord, teach us to pray" (Luke 11:1), was the heart cry of the disciples as they looked at Jesus who lived in perfect, unbroken communion with the living God. They knew they had much to learn from Him if they were to master the art of prayer. They knew that the Son of God, our great exemplar, was preeminently a man of prayer. He often rose up long before it was day and went out into a mountain alone to pray. Repeatedly we see Christ in a lonely mountain place at night spending long hours of solitude with His Father.

Have you learned the art of prayer? Many of us have not learned it as we ought. Yet the greatest of God's men and women have always been men and women who have learned the art of prayer. How did they learn the art? How can you learn the art?

Mastering the Art of Prayer

First of all, you must have a desire to learn. Secondly, you need an instructor. The Lord Jesus Christ is the master teacher of the art of prayer.

You will also need a textbook. You will find the Scriptures are the perfect source of instruction in this matter of prayer. It is important to understand that prayer is not based upon your own private concept of prayer, but rather on certain definite principles found in the Bible. And the Bible has a great deal to say about prayer.

Finally, you must be persistent and persevere to master the art of prayer. Someone once said, "If you will just spend a little time each day doing most anything, in due process you will become an expert at it." It doesn't matter in what field it is; you can learn more than most if you will stick with it every day, and this applies to prayer.

Practice makes perfect, so practice what you learn as you learn it. Prayer may seem awkward or difficult for you at first, but soon it will become as natural as breathing—and this is exactly as it should be for the Christian!

The Elements of Prayer

Prayer consists of certain basic elements. Certainly one of the most basic elements is *confession*. We come before an all-holy God whose eyes are so pure that He "canst not look on iniquity" (Hab. 1:13). Therefore, we must approach Him by confessing our sins and recognizing our unworthiness to even come into His presence. Isaiah, the prophet realized that he was a "man of unclean lips" only when he had seen God (Isa. 6:5). Before God can begin to work in our lives, we must confess to Him all that is out of focus within us. And He has promised to cleanse us "from all unrighteousness" when we do so (1 John 1:9).

The second element of prayer is *thanksgiving,* thanking God for all that He has done for us. Thankfulness in prayer can change the attitude of the soul. from sour to sweet. There is a sense, of course, in which we should have a holy discontent with our own spiritual progress, always seeking to be more mature and stronger in the Lord.

Yet, too often our discontent stems from a dissatisfaction with our lot in life, with our material circumstances or the situations in which we find ourselves, rather than with our lack of spiritual maturity or progress. We who are complacent about our souls give evidence of this when we complain about some physical or material thing which we lack. How poverty-stricken are such souls. What a blessing it is to know a holy contentment with our lot in life while yet having a holy discontent with our spiritual state.

So many people, because of the emptiness of their souls, are constantly grasping and reaching out for other things—position, wealth, status, possessions—not realizing that "things" will never fill that emptiness within. "Within every human heart," Blaise Pascal said, "there is a God-shaped vacuum, and naught can fill it but God alone."

As St. Augustine put it so many centuries ago, "Thou has made us for Thyself, and our hearts are restless until they find their rest in Thee." Yet how few people today have a thankfulness and a holy contentment about their lives. The person who can be content with anything—or nothing—in any situation is the person who can truly find peace with God. And the person who is truly thankful for what God has done for him can expect God to do "exceeding abundantly above all" that he asks or thinks (Eph. 3:20). God grant to each of us a holy discontentment and a true spirit of thankfulness.

The third element of prayer is *petition*. We are to ask God for things for ourselves. Any lawful, reasonable, honest need is a request to be made in prayer. It is not wrong to bring physical needs to God in prayer, as He is concerned for the very hairs on our heads. (See Matt. 10:30.) However, as progress is made in the art of prayer, you will notice that your requests begin to concern spiritual matters more and more. Why? Because as prayer becomes a regular habit, we learn quickly that God can take care of our physical needs without our asking. He knows that we "have need of these things" (Luke 12:30) and supplies them willingly and lovingly. But spiritual growth must be a desire that stems from us before God can grant it. He will not force spiritual maturity on the believer unless the believer desires and asks for it.

A fourth element of prayer is *intercession,* praying for others. This is the "college" level in the school of prayer in which we begin to pray for others. True intercession on behalf of others is achieved only after much time is spent with the Lord.

Jesus was the Great Intercessor for others, and we are to pray for others just as He did. The needs of this world are vast, yet how much do you really pray for others? How much do you agonize in prayer for those who are lost and needy all around you? When did you last weep for someone else, even for someone you say you love? "He that goeth forth and weepeth, bearing precious seed, shall doubtless come again with rejoicing, bringing his sheaves with him" (Psalm 126:6).

Pray for your minister. Pray for those who have the rule over you. Pray for your employers. Pray for your family. Pray for your friends. And pray for your enemies. Pray also for lost people with whom you rub shoulders each day. Pray each day that they will come to discover what you have already discovered. And as you see God answer your prayers in others' lives, you will know the joy of having interceded for His glory.

The fifth element of prayer is *adoration,* probably the least exercised form of prayer. Adoration is not merely thanking God for what He has given you, as in thanksgiving; it is praising Him for who He is. Do you marvel at the fact that the Creator of the universe wants you to talk to Him? That he loves you completely and unreservedly? That He gave His Son to die for you so that you might spend eternity with Him? Do you stand in awe of God's holiness, His purity, His love? You do? Then adore Him in your prayers; let your prayers be prayers of adoration.

These, then, are the five elements in prayer: confession, thanksgiving, petition, intercession, and adoration. Once you have learned to include each element in your prayer life, you will find an amazing new power and precision in your time spent alone in communion with God.

Conditions for Prayer

The Bible also lays down certain conditions for prayer. Without our meeting these conditions our prayers will be hindered or ineffectual. First of all, we must have a right relationship with God before we can expect that your prayers will be heard and answered. This means that we must be persons who are saved, not lost. Before God can grant us our requests, we must be His children, not children of the devil.

There is not just one great family in this world, as some would have us believe. There are two—those who are the children of God and those who are the children of Satan. Remember when Jesus rebuked the Pharisees and said of them, "Ye are of your father the devil" (John 8:44). The only prayer God can hear and answer from the lost person is the prayer of repentance and faith in Jesus Christ, the prayer that leads to salvation. That person is then adopted, by faith in Christ, into the family of God and has the right as a son of God to ask his heavenly Father for all his needs.

So first, you must be adopted into the family of God—born again into His family. You must be regenerated, justified, repenting of your sins and, by faith, receiving Jesus Christ into your heart. Then and only then do you enter into that right relationship with God and become His child. Without having accepted Jesus Christ, God's Son, as our Saviour, you and I remain outside the family of God. We remain at enmity with God (see Romans 5:10), outlaws and rebels against heaven.

Why should we expect God to answer our prayers if we continue to rebel against Him by rejecting the gift of salvation and sonship He has already offered us? It is like John Dillinger, that fugitive gangster, calling the police to complain about someone making noise next door and demanding that the authorities do something about it. Being a criminal himself, he is without right to make requests of the law. The police would have only one message for such as Dillinger: "Surrender. Give yourself up." And that is exactly what God says to that one still lost in his sins. "Surrend to Me. Give yourself up to My will. Then, as your Father, I will listen to your requests and answer your prayers."

Secondly, we must have a right relationship with others if we are to know a vital, powerful prayer life. The Bible says that "if thou bring thy gift to the altar, and there rememberest that thy brother hath aught against thee; leave there thy gift before the altar, and go thy way; first be reconciled to thy brother, and then come and offer thy gift" (Matt. 5:23,24). This is particularly true in our families. Husband, if you are out of harmony with your wife, the Bible says your prayers will be hindered (see 1 Peter 3:7). And that goes for wives as well (see Eph. 5:20-25; Col. 3:17-19). When all is well between you and your family, between you and your friends and acquaintances, then you can expect your prayer life to thrive.

Thirdly, we must be free of unconfessed sin, if we want God to hear our prayers. The Bible says, "If I regard iniquity in my heart, the Lord will not hear me" (Psalm 66:18). If we harbor any secret sins in our hearts and are unwilling to repent of them and forsake them, God plainly says He will not hear us. Unconfessed sin will always close God's ears to our prayers, just as confession will remove hindrances to our prayer life.

Fourthly, when we pray we must ask in faith. The Bible says, "But let him ask in faith, nothing wavering: for he that wavereth is like a wave of the sea driven with the wind and tossed. For let not that man think that he shall receive anything of the Lord" (James 1:6,7). Of course, our faith does not have to be monumental in order for God to answer. Jesus said that even faith the size of a grain of mustard seed would accomplish great things in the Kingdom of God. (See Matt. 17:20.) But the person who prays and who doubts God even as he is praying will not see the miracles of God that great faith is capable of producing. (See Matt. 9:29.) Yet as we see God answering our prayers, our faith increases, so that the next thing we pray for requires more holy boldness, more trust on our part. And the answer, in turn, invariably reveals an equal measure more of God's power and might.

Finally, we must ask according to God's will. We cannot expect our heavenly Father to give us everything that we ask for. And, indeed, it is good that He does not, for most of us do not even know what to ask Him for. What chaos there would be, if God were to grant all the requests His children make in prayer. Yet we have the assurance that when we have asked according to His will, the answer is forthcoming. (See 1 John 5:14,15.) As a Christian, you will have power in prayer when you can honestly pray, "Not my will, but thine, be done" (Luke 22:42).

Obstacles to Prayer

We have now studied the five aspects or elements of prayer and the five conditions of prayer. Now let us look at five obstacles to prayer, five snares that prevent Christians from exercising their God-given right and privilege to come to the Father and commune with Him in prayer.

Perhaps the greatest obstacle to prayer is unbelief. We just do not believe that God will answer our prayers. Perhaps this lack of faith stems from prayers which we have made and which were not answered because, in our ignorance of the scriptural criteria for prayer, they were not in God's will or what He knew we needed at the time. Even those who see immediate and definite answers to prayer often have trouble believing God the next time they go to Him in prayer. It is as if our human nature automatically doubts God. And when we do doubt, He cannot perform the miraculous as He would like to.

Another obstacle to prayer is carnality—a failure to be the spiritual people God meant us as Christians to be. Christians who have never formed the habit of prayer are carnal Christians. Usually they are also the same Christians who never go to church, never pay any attention to God, never obey the least of His commandments . . . until suddenly they need Him. An illness, a problem in the home, the loss of a job—any of these things might turn that person to God in prayer. Of course, God in His grace will still love that person and care for him, but the carnal Christian's prayer life is never what it should or can be.

A third obstacle to prayer is insincerity. This means not being absolutely honest with God and with yourself. It means not having your heart in your prayers. Have you ever found yourself praying by rote, not really caring about what you were asking God for, but doing it rather out of a sense of duty and obligation? This is insincerity, and it is a great hindrance to one's prayer life. When you pray, be ruthlessly honest with yourself and with God.

A fourth obstacle to prayer is a lack of discipline. If we have a teacher, a textbook, and know the basic principles of any art, we must then set a definite time each day for practice. It is not enough for a child to run past a piano and tinkle a few notes; he must sit down and practice daily. It is the same with prayer. The lack of daily discipline is why so few people make any progress in their prayer lives and why so few are really men and women of prayer. Prayer should begin in the morning ("Give us this day our daily bread" is hardly a prayer to be saved until night!), and progress throughout the day. It should also be one of the last things we do at night.

People who say they can't pray aloud use this as an excuse to cover up the fact that they can't pray at all. Any man or woman who diligently spends much time in prayer alone, unless he is mute, can pray aloud. The person who can't pray aloud is a person who has no real closeted time of prayer, who has not learned the secrets of prayer in private.

The finaly obstacle to prayer is lack of practice, a lack of progressive practice of prayer. A paino student has a whole set of music books. He begins with the most elemental and then goes on to the most difficult piece of music. He cannot play the same tune over and over again and expect to grow in the art. But this is exactly what happens to many people in prayer. There are those who have been Christians for years and years and yet still pray the same little prayer over and over again. There is no progress in their life, no stretching of their souls. In order to grow in the art of prayer, you need to practice progressive prayer; you need to step out and up to higher levels of prayer as you mature in Christ.

To be really proficient in the art of prayer is the most noble, the most needed, and the most difficult of arts. It is also, however, the most rewarding, for God greatly answers prayer. The English poet and author, Alfred Lord Tennyson, said "More things are wrought by prayer than this world dreams of." How true this is! Recently in a week of prayer here in our church we prayed to God that ten people would give their lives for full-time Christian service in the coming year. On December 30, someone called long distance to tell me he had decided to go into full-time Christian work. He was the tenth person for that year! God does indeed answer the prayers of His children!

How much you miss when you do not pray! Suppose the president of our country sent you a personal letter saying that he was concerned about your welfare and wanted to help you. Suppose he had placed at your disposal in a national bank a vast sum of money to provide for all your needs. He said he was also making all the powers of his office available to you as well. Would you spurn such an offer? Of course not!

Yet many of us have spurned a far more wonderful offer from the God of the universe, who invites us to come and "take the water of life freely" (Rev. 22:17). Ask of Him who freely gives, for He is ready and able to provide for all our needs out of His unsearchable, unlimited riches.

As you learn the art of prayer, as you put roots down ever deeper into that unseen fountain of communion with the living God, you will find refreshment for your soul. And those same living waters will cause your Christian life to grow into new, exciting and infinite dimensions. The Bible—God's Word—and the God of the Bible who hears and answers prayer promises it to you!

When I Speak to God 4

In *Pilgrim's Progress,* John Bunyan's great allegory of the Christian life, we see the pilgrim, Christian, making his way from the City of Destruction to the Celestial City by way of that hill upon which stand three crosses. In a journey full of ups and downs, Christian falls into the Slough of Despond, climbs the Delectable Mountains, encounters the Giant Despair, molders in the dungeon of the giant's Doubting Castle and stands trial in Vanity Fair.

At one point in his pilgrimage, Christian is ascending the Hill Difficulty. Night falls before he is able to reach the top, so he stops at the Palace Beautiful by the roadside in hopes of obtaining accommodation for the night. Watchful, the porter of the lodge, guides Christian past the two chained lions guarding the palace and takes him in, explaining to Christian that the palace was built by the Lord of the hill "for the relief and security of pilgrims" such as Christian.

Christian sojourns two days at the Palace Beautiful. On the morning of the second day, before his departure, he is outfitted from head to foot in armor by his four hostesses, Discretion, Prudence, Piety and Charity. This armor, provided by the Lord of the hill, is to protect Christian from "assaults in the way" as he continues his journey. It consists of "sword, shield, helmet, breastplate, all-prayer, and shoes that would not wear out."

Soon after descending the Hill Difficulty, Christian enters the Valley of Humiliation where he is ambushed by "a foul fiend," Apollyon. "Prepare thyself to die," Apollyon says as he attacks Christian. "Here will I spill thy soul." Safe in the Lord's armor, Christian wards off Apollyon's blows with his shield and mortally wounds his adversary with his sword. Apollyon then flees from Christian leaving him free to go on his way.

Christian next enters the Valley of the Shadow of Death. He "must needs go through it, because the way to the Celestial City lay through the midst of it." But there in the midst of this valley, "hard by the wayside" and covering some "several miles together," was the mouth of hell. Christian realized he had to pass this fearsome place.

"Now, thought Christian, what shall I do? And ever and anon the flame and smoke would come out in such abundance, with sparks and hideous noises (things that cared not for Christian's sword, as did Apollyon before), that he was forced to put up his sword, and betake himself to another weapon, called all-prayer."* Armed with the weapon "called all-

---

* John Bunyan, *The Pilgrim's Progress* (New York: Thomas Nelson and Sons, Ltd.), p. 67.

prayer," Christian passed safely around the mouth of hell and through the Valley of the Shadow of Death.

The Power of All-Prayer

I will never forget the first time that I read *Pilgrim's Progress* and came across those curious words "all-prayer," which Bunyan had hyphenated to give them a heightened effect. Yet Bunyan was not the first to use the words "all prayer." Rather, he borrowed them from the apostle Paul who speaks of "all-prayer" in his epistle to the Ephesians.

In Ephesians 6:10-18, Paul tells us that as Christians we are to "put on the whole armor of God." He then describes this accouterment as "having your loins girt about with truth, and having on the breastplate of righteousness; and your feet shod with the preparation of the gospel of peace; above all, taking the shield of faith, wherewith ye shall be able to quench all the fiery darts of the wicked. And take the helmet of salvation, and the sword of the Spirit, which is the word of God" (Eph. 6:14-17). Then finally, says Paul, do this "praying always with all prayer and supplication in the Spirit" (Eph. 6:18).

Is all-prayer a part of the armor of the Christian? It is not, and herein lies its true significance. Notice that in the text we have just quoted, there is no part of the armor named to correspond specifically to all-prayer. Rather Paul speaks of prayer *after* he tells the Christian to "put on the whole armor of God" (Eph. 6:11) and *after* he names all the parts of this armor. After all this he tells the Christian to be "praying always with all prayer." Prayer is the oil that lubricates the Christian's armor.

What is Paul really saying here? In effect, he is saying that we are not only to take the armor of God, but we are also to take with us the God of the armor. However fully equipped we may be with the armor of God, however complete may be our protection, however sharp may be our sword, we are not yet ready to venture into the battle until we call the General to lead us forth. He alone can captain the well-fought fight. Without His presence, without His leading, all of our armor will simply be so much added weight to bear. It will only weigh us down as Saul's armor weighed David down. We can wear the armor well only when empowered by all-prayer. "Praying always with all prayer."

Remember that Paul has told us as Christians to put on the *whole* armor of God. Yet the trouble with many Christians is that they put on only *part* of that armor. And tragically for many, such half measures have resulted in full destruction. There are those who think they have put on the breastplate of righteousness, yet their prayers go unuttered. There are others who suppose themselves shod with the preparation of the gospel, yet they do not pray. Still others glory in their strong hold on the sword of the Spirit—"which is the word of God"—or rejoice in having taken the helmet of salvation, but yet they remain prayerless. There are even those who have taken that helmet, who have learned how to wield that sword, who have shod their feet, who have put on the whole armor of God. But because such a one wears it day in and day out, never oiling it with all-prayer, all that armor only rusts on the wearer. Unoiled by all-prayer, the rusted-over armor leaves the Christian defenseless, and he battles in vain. He has no hope of victory who fights the foe unequipped or unprepared. The true Christian soldier goes forth in full armor, fully lubricated by the oil of prayer. He goes forth wearing the "whole armor of God" *and* "praying always with all prayer."

Praying Always

When and how are we to use this power of all-prayer? "Praying always with all prayer," replies the apostle Paul. Notice the command to pray always. The verbs used by Paul in this passage from Ephesians are in the imperative mood in the original Greek. This means they are commandments, not mere requests. In other words, Paul is telling us that "praying always" is a basic requirement, not an option, of the Christian life.

Many Christians are astonished to learn that the Bible tells us to pray always. Thoughout the New Testament it says this in many ways: "Pray without ceasing" (1 Thess. 5:17) "giving thanks always for all things" (Eph. 5:20), "praying always for you" (Col. 1:3). We should give thanks for every blessing, every good thing, and, yes, even for every tragedy and mishap that befalls us. Why? Because if we are Christ's, we know that whatever happens does so because our heavenly Father allows it to happen. He turns it all to our good, using it to fashion us more and more in His own image. In this way He causes the doors within us to be consumed and our gold to be refined.

Yet there are some Christians who not only do not pray always, they never pray at all. There are others who perhaps in dire emergencies, who during some of the more terrible tragedies of life, may utter a prayer to the God they have previously ignored. Still others go to their knees occasionally in prayer. But most of us are far from "praying always with all prayer."

We should meet every temptation with prayer. We should enjoy every proper amusement with prayer. We should encounter every obstacle with prayer. We should receive every setback with prayer. We should endeavor in every task to succeed by prayer. And we should meet every person with prayer that the Spirit of God in us might manifest the love and joy and peace of Christ to them. "Praying always with all prayer."

All Manner of Prayer

Paul says to pray always "with all prayer and supplication." The term "all prayer" can also be translated "all kinds of prayer" or "all manner of prayer." When Paul told us to "put on the whole armor of God," he also told us to pray always "with all prayer." Why? Because just as there are Christians who put on only part of God's armor, leaving off the rest, so there are Christians who come to prayer, taking only a certain part and leaving off all the rest. Neither the armory of the Lord nor the throne of prayer is a cafeteria to which Christians can come, selecting that which suits their fancy and omitting that which does not.

As God's children praying to our heavenly Father, we must learn the art of "praying always with all prayer," with "all kinds of prayer" or "all manner of prayer." And the Scripture teaches that there are all kinds and manner of prayer.

First, there is the *ejaculatory prayer,* that type of prayer which we hurtle heavenward like speedy telegrams in times of sudden emergency. And this is good, these requests for immediate aid. Such prayer alarms call down heaven's help upon urgent and immediate needs here below.

You hear the wailing of a siren and you see the approach of flashing red lights, as an ambulance draws near and then disappears around the corner where you stand. Does a prayer shoot forth from your heart to heaven for this one in obvious dire need? How many Christians will that ambulance pass without anyone lifting eyes and heart heavenward in prayer, appealing for divine intervention in the life of the one lying within?

You see a person by the roadside in trouble, trying to fix his car. Do you stop? Or, if you can't stop, do you send up that instantaneous prayer on his behalf that he will be helped? And do you also pray that if this person does not already know Jesus Christ as Saviour, God will reveal Himself to him? Whatever may be the need, we shoud pray. And the ejaculatory prayer is one which we should utter many times each day as we see immediate needs all around us.

Then there is *closeted prayer,* that time of prayer when we get down on our knees alone with the Lord. It should be scheduled every day, for unless scheduled it will not come to pass. You may prefer a time of prayer immediately before or after your personal Bible study. I personally prefer to pray in the morning. "My voice shalt thou hear in the morning, O

Lord," writes the Psalmist. "In the morning will I direct my prayer unto thee, and will look up" (Psalm 5:3).

I tremble to think of beginning a day without beginning with God, of undertaking the work assigned to me without the help of the Almighty. There are some who might suppose this to be weakness on my part, and they would be right, for I am human and weak and poor and needy. Yes, it is weakness, but God can make the weak strong. His strength is made perfect in our weakness. (See 2 Cor. 12:9.) With Paul I can say, "Most gladly therefore will I rather glory in my infirmities, that the power of Christ may rest upon me" (2 Cor. 12:9).

But whether you choose to pray in the morning or evening or any other time, faithfully keep this daily time of close communion with God. One of the great battles of Christian life is to maintain closet time, this quiet time alone with the Lord when everything else is set aside. Many people are quite willing to pray if they can be doing something else at the same time. Someone told me recently that he often prayed when he was shaving or driving along in his car. Although this is possible, there should still be that time set aside only for prayer.

A real test of our faith is our willingness to set aside time each day to pray with the Lord no matter what other things we have to do. Martin Luther regularly prayed two hours each day. But when he had an exceptionally busy day, he increased his personal prayer time to three hours. He knew that when he had a lot to get done, he couldn't do it without more help from God. He knew better than to try and change the world alone.

Thirdly, there is the *concerted* or *group prayer*. Every once in a while I meet a babe in Christ who had read only two books in the Bible and has come to the conclusion that prayer meetings are sinful because Jesus said to go into the closet and pray. (See Matt. 6:6.) I just smile and know that eventually they are going to read more and find out that it was —and still is—the custom of the people of God to join together.

Jesus has told us that wherever two or three believers are gathered together in His name, He is there in the midst of them (See Matt. 18:20.) And if these believers agree on what they are asking God for, He has promised that it shall come to pass (Matt. 18:19). The saints of God have met together throughout the week since the founding of the church to recharge their spiritual batteries and to support one another in their prayers.

Lastly, there is what is known as *continual prayer*. This is the prayer "without ceasing" (1 Thess. 5:17). It is that constant communion between the individual and his Saviour that is achieved by only the most faithful and diligent of Christians. Isn't it wonderful that our Lord is never too busy for us! Throughout the day, wherever we might be, we can be in communion with Him—a communion that will enrich our lives and bless our hearts as well as blessing those around us.

This communion of continual prayer can utterly transform our lives. The prayer of thanksgiving can instantly dispel all of those little irritations, annoyances, disturbances, disappointments and grievances in our daily lives. The prayer of praise can make us more aware of who God is and how His grace has overflowed upon us. The prayer of request can make known to us His immense power and His willingness to help no matter how small the detail of our lives may seem.

How to Pray

These are the kinds of prayer included in the words "all prayer." But *how* are we to pray? There are two important keys here: we are *to pray in the Spirit of God,* and we are *to pray with all perseverance.*

Praying in the Spirit means that we are to realize that Jesus Christ has come by His Spirit into our hearts and that He will help us to pray. "The Spirit itself maketh intercession for us with groanings which cannot be uttered . . . according to the will of God" (Rom. 8:26,27). We are to pray knowing that the Holy Spirit will take our prayers and present them to God. We are to pray surrendered unto Christ, with our lives open to the Spirit of God to take over completely.

And we are to pray with perseverance. Was there a time in the past when you prayed better and with more persistence than you do now? This happens to many of us, for it is all too easy to pray once for something and then forget about it. We need to persevere in prayer. But how many of us are willing to get down on our knees day after day, week after week, even year after year to see God's miracles being done? How many of us have the dedication and faith necessary to pray with perseverance, to persevere in all-prayer?

Paul told the Ephesians to be "praying always with all prayer and . . . with all perseverance" (Eph. 6:18). Most of us grow weary of praying for something when the answer does not come immediately according to our own timetable. But the Scriptures teach that the saint who can pray with perseverance is the one who will see the great works of God done all around him.

Pray for Others

For what or whom should we persevere in prayer. Notice that when Paul tells us to be "praying always with all prayer," he also adds the words "with all perseverance and supplications for all saints" (Eph. 6:18). Everyone who truly knows Christ as Lord and Saviour is a saint. Every person sanctified by His Spirit is a saint. Every Christian is a saint. And every saint stands in the need of the prayers of other saints.

Do you pray for all the saints? Do you as a Christian really pray for other Christians as you ought? Do you persevere in prayer for them, supplicating for them, holding them up by name, praying for them faithfully and specifically according to their needs? "Praying always with all prayer . . . for all saints."

Pray for Yourself

Note that even as he requests us to persevere in prayer for others, Paul was himself in great personal need. He was a prisoner in Rome, in a dank, cold, subterranean dungeon carved out of stone beneath the floor of the city's infamous Mammertine Prison.

Paul was lowered by rope through a small hole in the prison floor into his cave-like cell where he remained for two years without ever seeing the light of day.

Yet Paul did not pray for release. He did not pray for any improvement in his own situation. Rather, he requested that we persevere in prayer "and supplication for all saints." And only then did he request prayer for himself. And what did he ask for? "And (pray) for me, that utterance may be given unto me, that I may open my mouth boldly, to make known the mystery of the gospel, for which I am an ambassador in bonds; that therein I may speak boldly, as I ought to speak" (Eph. 6:19, 20).

Even though in prison, Paul knew he was there as God's ambassador in bonds, and he prayed only that his mouth might be opened boldly to proclaim the gospel of Christ. When you pray for yourself, what do you ask God for? Learn, like Paul, to persevere in prayer," "praying always with all prayer and . . . with all perseverance," for all saints and their welfare first, then for yourself and your witness.

"Praying always with all prayer." How easy it is to talk about prayer. And how hard it is to actually pray, much less to persevere in it. But neglect the practice of all-prayer, and you neglect to oil the armor provided you by a loving Lord. We gladly wrap ourselves in the whole of the armor of God, yet only with difficulty do we take time to oil it and keep it in fighting trim with the lubricant of all-prayer. Remember, when we allow our prayers to go before us into the daily battle of life, we go forth with the armor of God protecting us and the God of the armor leading us. "Praying always with all prayer."

I Speak
to God in
Faith

5

When you and I come to the end of this pilgrimage, if we look back with perceptive eyes over all the days God has given us here below, we will see that all our life here has simply been a walk of faith in the promises of God. Is this a new thought for you? If it is, let it get hold of your mind, for it could revolutionize your life. I have no question of its validity, "being fully persuaded that, what he had promised, he was able also to perform" (Rom. 4:21).

The Evidence of God's Promises

Nature itself is eloquent testimony to the truthfulness of God's promises. Thousands of years ago, after the Flood God promised that "while the earth remaineth, seedtime and harvest, and cold and heat, and summer and winter, and day and night shall not cease" (Gen. 8:22). God promised that season would follow season in regular succession until the end of the world. And so Spring comes forth each year bearing in her arms the waking infant of nature. She is followed by Summer adorning her hair with flowers. After her comes Fall with vines entwining his legs and arms and with corn on his back. Finally, shaking with frost, comes old man Winter. And each year as they come, they place one hand on the broad table of nature, raise the other hand to the sky and solemnly affirm that the promises of God are true.

History is one long unfolding of the promises of God; He is doing exactly what He said He would do. The whole history of the people of Israel is one huge picture-book record of God's promises to His people. Yes, I believe that all of this world—everything that goes on here beneath the sun—is simply the unraveling of the promises.

"But," you ask, "what of all the unpleasant things going on around us—all sorts of terrible things?" Let me tell you that what you are seeing worked out even in the problems and miseries around us is simply the unraveling of the promises of God.

God's Promises Are Conditional

Remember that many of God's promises are conditional. God has promised to people exactly what would happen to them under certain given conditions. He promised them that if they did certain things, he would cause or allow certain things to happen to them. For instance, God promised Adam and Eve that if they ate of the tree of the knowledge of good and evil which stood in the midst of the Garden of Eden "thou shalt surely die" (Gen. 2:17). They ate, and they died. It was the fulfillment of the promise of God.

God's Promises Are True

Everything that happens can be seen to be the promises of God coming true, whether for blessing or for cursing. For some, this is a frightening thought. But if you are a Christian, a new creature in Christ, regenerated by the Spirit of God and redeemed by the Son of God, then the promises of God should be exceedingly precious to you. The Scripture says there "are given unto us exceeding great and precious promises" (2 Pet. 1:4). These promises are blank checks signed by God and given to us.

The Promises of God Are Yours

Do you believe the promises of God? "Why, certainly I believe the promises of God," you say. But I say you don't believe. Why? Because if you really believed them you would be claiming them; you would be cashing them and spending them.

Do you claim the promises of God? You prove that you believe the promises of God by claiming them. You see, to cash these checks, to claim these promises, you must appropriate them by faith. And God has pledged Himself to fulfill them, if only we ask in faith. Don't go along through life as a spiritual pauper when you can and should be spiritually rich. Knowing and believing that God stands firmly behind what He has said in His Word can mean the difference between a prayer life that sees miracles and one that is empty and shallow.

Do you pray the promises of God? If not, why not? You really have no reason to believe that the answer to your prayers will be anything other than that which He has promised.

66

Do you learn His promises? I wonder. For months in the Sunday evening services here in our church, we have been learning together the promises of God. But yet some of the people in our church only sit there like bumps on a log. They don't bother to learn the promises of God, much less to believe them or to pray them. So how can they expect me to believe that they believe them. I'm not impressed.

Suppose you are in desperate financial need and someone who knows of your need writes you a check more than covering the amount needed. He gives you the check and assures you that it is good. You thank him and say, "Oh, I believe you. I know it's a good check." But then you just let it lie around, day after day, month after month, covered up, forgotten, un-cashed, unspent. The first thing your friend would conclude is that you didn't believe the check was any good after all. A farfetched example? Not at all, for it clearly illustrates the attitude many people have concerning the promises of God. Yet we know that what He has promised He is "able also to perform" (Rom. 4:21). All of God's promises are yea and amen in Jesus Christ.

Someone once said that if any individual would spend every day for one month studying the promises of God so as to learn them, and then believing and praying them, the whole of their lives would be changed. Their fear would be changed to courage, their timidity to confidence, their discouragement to a bright outlook for the future.

Isn't it amazing that God should condescend to give us promises at all? No earthly judge makes deals with those who do not deserve them. And yet this is exactly what God does. We never deserve any of His promises, and yet He richly bestows them upon us. When they are received by faith, nothing in heaven or earth can take them away from us.

Receiving God's Promises

Have you received the promises of God? Let us start with the most important promise of all. Here it is: God offers to you eternal life. He promises eternal life to you, if you believe. "Whosoever believeth in him should not perish, but have eternal life" (John 3:15). "He that believeth on the Son hath everlasting life" (John 3:36).

"I give unto them eternal life; and they shall never perish," Jesus promised (John 10:28). Again He promised: "Whosoever liveth and believeth in me shall never die. Believest thou this?" (John 11:26).

"What must I do to be saved?" cried the trembling Philippian jailer on his knees as he looked up into the face of the apostle Paul (Acts 16:30).

The answer came back as a promise from heaven: "Believe on the Lord Jesus Christ, and thou shalt be saved, and thy house (Act 16:31).

Have you claimed that promise? Do you believe that promise? It is easy to know if you have received God's promise of eternal life. Just answer this question: "Are you saved?"

You say, "Well now, I don't know about that."

Then I say, "You don't believe the promise of God."

"Oh, but I do," you protest.

No you don't. It's simple. God freely offers you eternal life in Christ. Accept it. Receive it by faith.

68

But you say, "That's too simple."

Yes, it could not be simpler. God offers. You accept. God promises. You receive. Christ died for your sin, and if you will trust Him—take Him at His word and believe His promise—you will have eternal life.

Do you believe God? If you do, then you can say, "I know I'm saved and going to heaven." If you can't say those words then you don't believe God. More than that, you are calling God a liar for "he that believeth not God hath made him a liar; because he believeth not the record that God gave of his Son" (1 John 5:10). And what is the record? "This is the record, that God hath given to us eternal life, and this life is in his Son. He that hath the Son hath life" (1 John 5:11,12).

Do you trust in Christ alone? If you have trusted in Jesus Christ for your salvation, if you have put your whole hope in the cross of Christ and not in your own false works or self-righteousness, then you have His promise of eternal life. It is undeserved, unmerited, unearned and paid for by another. Nevertheless, you have God's promise: "God . . . gave his only begotten Son, that whosoever believeth in him should not perish, but have everlasting life" (John 3:16). Believe the promise. Receive eternal life.

But there is so much more. Jesus promises that anyone who comes to Him will be received. He promises us a loving welcome, a hearty reception. He says: "All that the Father giveth me shall come to me; and him that cometh to me I will in no wise cast out" (John 6:37).

You say, "I'm not fit to come to Christ. He won't receive me. I'm not good enough."

You are absolutely right—you're not good enough. But you are also absolutely wrong—He will receive you. Whether or not you are good enough has nothing to do with whether or not Jesus will receive you. We are accepted though we are entirely and totally unacceptable. We are accepted for Christ's sake, not for our own sake. Christ receiveth sinful men, for "him that cometh to me I will in no wise cast out."

I don't care what you are, I don't care what kind of business dealings you have been engaged in, I don't care what kind of cheating you have been doing on your wife or on your husband or in school, I don't care what kind of secret sin you are harboring. If you will come to Christ He will forgive you and transform you. He has promised to do it! He will in no wise cast you out!

Perhaps you have already come to Christ and received Him as Lord and Saviour. And He has received you. At first, you rejoiced in your salvation and things went well for awhile. Then you fell into some grievous sin and now you cannot even look up into His face. You hang your head. The fellowship with your Saviour is broken. You are no longer aware of His presence. You feel dirty, unclean, unworthy, foul. You cannot even go to Him in prayer.

What can you do? Remember, even here there is a promise for you to claim. Once Martin Luther felt that Satan was in his room, and Satan seemed to say to him, "Martin Luther, when you stand before the judgment, in that hour I will cause the whole world to know what your sins are, and everyone will know everything about you."

Luther responded. "Devil, you don't know the half of it. Why, I'm twice as bad as you think I am. But when you finish telling what you know, then I have a word to add, and it is this, 'The blood of Jesus Christ his Son cleanseth us from all sin' " (1 John 1:7).

Do you really think there is any sin you have committed that the Son of God cannot cleanse away? If so, then claim these promises: "Though your sins be as scarlet, they shall be as white as snow; though they be red like crimson, they shall be as wool" (Isa. 1:18); "As far as the east is from the west, so far hath he removed our transgressions from us" (Ps. 103:12); "thou wilt cast away their sins into the depths of the sea" (Mic. 7:19); "for I will forgive their iniquity, and I will remember their sin no more" (Jer. 31:34). God is willing to forget. His mercy is new each morning and fresh each day.

Perhaps you are weary; you are tired. There is a promise for you: "Come unto me, all ye that labour and are heavy laden, and I will give you rest" (Matt. 11:28). Come unto Him in prayer. Come unto Him in His Word. Come unto Him in meditation and Christ will give you rest.

Perhaps your problem is pride and arrogance, a self-inflated ego. Then claim this promise: "Take my yoke upon you, and learn of me; for I am meek and lowly in heart: and ye shall find rest unto your souls" (Matt. 11:29).

Perhaps you are troubled by a burden that is too heavy for you to carry by yourself. Receive Jesus' promise: "For my yoke is easy, and my burden is light" (Matt. 11:30).

Perhaps your need is that you are afraid of life. It

is more than you can handle, it is too big for you, you don't know what to do with it, you can't do anything right. You can't take care of your family properly, or school is towering over you and threatens to crush you, or your job has gotten to be too much for you. Here is a promise from the Word of God, and it has your name on it: "I can do all things through Christ which strengtheneth me" (Phil. 4:13).

Grasp that promise with both hands and hold tight to it. It does not mean self-confidence, for Scripture condemns man's confidence in man. "Thus saith the Lord; Cursed be the man that trusteth in man, and maketh flesh his arm" (Jer. 17:5). God offers you something greater than self-confidence; He promises you Christ-confidence, a confidence in the Son of God who dwells in the heart of the believer. "I can do *all* things through Christ. . . ."

There was a time when I was afraid of my own shadow. I could no more stand in a pulpit and preach than I could have flown on my own to the moon. But I began to take Christ at His Word. And now I even astonish myself today at some of the things I take on. But the Lord brings me through them. I don't care what it is, for I believe that "I can do *all* things through Christ which strengtheneth me." And do you know something else? I am not afraid of life anymore because He who has already won the victory over life —and death—dwells in my heart.

Are you concerned about your life? About what you should do? About decisions you have to make? Then "trust in the Lord with all thine heart; and lean not unto thine own understanding. In all thy ways acknowledge him, and he shall direct thy paths"

72

(Prov. 3:5,6); "I will instruct thee and teach thee in the way which thou shalt go: I will guide thee with mine eye" (Ps. 32:8). He promises to make your life rich and fruitful to guide your every step.

God promises us that we can be spiritually fruitful Christians; that He will fill us with His Spirit. And He will cause us to bear much fruit. "He that abideth in me, and I in him, the same bringeth forth much fruit: for without me ye can do nothing" (John 15:5). Oh, that we would learn to abide in His Word and to abide in Him in prayer and to walk in Him, claiming promises such as these for our lives.

Perhaps you are afraid to travel, to get on a plane? Then listen to these promises: "Behold, I am with thee, and will keep thee in all places whither thou goest" (Gen. 28:15); "Be strong and of a good courage; be not afraid, neither be thou dismayed: for the Lord thy God is with thee whithersoever thou goest" (Josh. 1:9).

Perhaps you have problems with other people, with enemies. Then claim this promise: "No weapon that is formed against thee shall prosper; and every tongue that shall rise against thee in judgment thou shalt condemn. This is the heritage of the servants of the Lord, and their righteousness is of me, saith the Lord" (Isa. 54:17).

Perhaps you are fearful or lonely. Here is God's promise to you: "I will never leave thee, nor forsake thee. . . . The Lord is my helper and I will not fear what man shall do unto me" (Heb. 13:5,6). If you are a Christian, and you know that Christ is with you and in you, then you can claim even this promise when you come to that last dark valley known as death: "Yea, though I walk through the valley of the shadow of death, I will fear no evil: for thou art with me; thy rod and thy staff they comfort me" (Ps. 23:4).

Perhaps you are overwhelmed by circumstances. Remember, God has promised that He will work all things "together for good to them that love God, to them who are the called according to his purpose" (Rom. 8:28). If we would just claim this promise, that whatever comes to us comes through the filter of a Father's love and that He will change it by the amazing alchemy of His grace to our own good, how much easier life would be for us!

We have so many wonderful promises of prayer: "And all things, whatsoever ye shall ask in prayer, believing, ye shall receive" (Matt. 21:22); "And this is the confidence that we have in him, that, if we ask any thing according to his will, he heareth us: and if we know that he hear us, whatsoever we ask, we know that we have the petitions that we desired of him" (1 John 5:14,15); "And it shall come to pass, that before they call, I will answer; and while they are yet speaking, I will hear" (Isa. 65:24).

And God has promised even more than that! He has promised to do so much for us that our minds cannot even begin to comprehend all that He has in store for us! "Call unto me, and I will answer thee, and shew thee great and mighty things, which thou knowest not" (Jer. 33:3). Yes, God promises us that in Christ there is available to us that which we haven't even thought of.

Our God is the God of the great surprise. "Eye hath not seen, nor ear heard, neither have entered

74

into the heart of man, the things which God hath prepared for them that love him" (1 Cor. 2:9).

Are you yet fully persuaded that what God has promised, He is able to perform? May God grant to you and to me a belief in His Word—that leather-bound checkbook given to us by God. Might we by faith cash those promises given us by Him who has promised to supply all of our needs "according to his riches in glory by Christ Jesus" (Phil. 4:19) that we might live here below, not as spiritual paupers, but as royal princes and princesses, the sons and daughters of the King of kings.

When
God
Answers

6

It was almost Thanksgiving and a first-grade class was discussing the meaning of gratitude. The teacher asked if the students knew what the word meant. After some moments a little boy raised his hand and said, "Gratitude is the memory of the heart." I think this is a pretty good definition of gratitude. But for the moment let us look at the counterpart of gratitude: ingratitude. For it seems that most of us have short memories. If the memory of our minds is short, the memory of our hearts seems even shorter.

A friend of mine was wandering rather aimlessly one day along the Gaza Road. His thoughts were elsewhere for he was daydreaming and not paying any particular attention to the scenery around him. He was brought back to reality with a sharp jolt when he suddenly found himself in the midst of a band of filthy beggars. A dozen or more of them clothed in the most hideous rags were standing around him. They were hairless, eyeless and noseless. They lifted fingerless hands before his face and waved handless arms in the air. They cried out to him with gurgling sounds coming from throats eaten out by leprosy. "I was horrified," he said.

The tragedy and horror of leprosy was even more familiar in Jesus' day. In his Gospel, Luke relates how just such a sight as this met the eyes of our Saviour one day, as He approached a small village on His way from the north of Palestine to Golgotha. Jesus was confronted by ten lepers, outcasts of society, whom the Mosaic Law had removed from their fellowmen to prevent the spread of their disease.

Lepers of that day were confined to a walking death, required always to cry out, "Unclean, unclean," and to approach no closer than a hundred paces to any healthy person. The ten lepers saw Jesus and called Him by name, "Jesus, Master, have mercy on us" (Luke 17:13). They had known of His miraculous cures and of other lepers like themselves whom He had healed. They knew He was their last hope, their last chance for wholeness, for already the disease had ravaged their bodies, causing other people to turn away from them in horror and disgust.

In answer to their cry, Jesus responded, "Go shew yourselves unto the priests" (Luke 17:14). That was all. There is no record that the lepers ever got closer to Jesus than the stipulated hundred paces, so He probably never touched them. Nor was any more said between them. He spoke only the one sentence to the lepers. They then turned and left, and that was all there was to the lepers' brief encounter with the Saviour.

But that was not all that happened to the lepers. In departing to go to the priests, they obeyed Christ's command, thereby showing they had faith in His ability to heal. For they knew what Jesus meant about going to the priests; they knew that the priests were the only men who could declare them cleansed of the leprosy.

As they were walking along, suddenly there was a sudden surge of something in their bodies, a throb of new life, a thrill of vitality. Their dragging limbs were quickened, their whitened flesh was changed, various parts of their bodies that had been sloughed off long ago were reformed . . . and they knew that they had been cleansed!

And now we come to the point of the whole narrative. One of the cleansed lepers, a Samaritan (half Jew and half Gentile), turned around and went back to Christ, glorifying God as he went. And when he reached Jesus, he fell on his face at the Saviour's feet and gave Him thanks for the cure that had been wrought upon him. The other nine cleansed lepers? We never hear from them or about them again.

Now this is a brief incident but I believe that it has much meaning for us today. Most of us, I think, look upon our lack of failure to be thankful as a rather minor sin, not as one of the major transgressions. In fact, we almost take ingratitude for granted, don't we, because we're so accustomed to it.

The Bible, however, presents ingratitude in a very different light. In the first chapter of Romans, Paul is cataloging the sins and corruptions of the heathen world of which we were once a part before salvation. He describes many base and vile depravities, but if you trace them back to their source, you find: "Because that, when they knew God, they glorified him not as God, neither were thankful" (Rom. 1:21). And so God gave them up!

Why did God create the world? He created it for His own glory. What is the chief end of man? It is to glorify God and enjoy Him forever. And so the Bible presents thanklessness as an astounding vice, a corruptible sin and a source of many of the corruptions of the heathen world.

Now let us go back to the lepers in the incident in Luke. What kind of men were they? What kind of ingrates would ignore the God who had so wonderfully and graciously healed their sick and dying bodies? Heathen men, no doubt, you are saying. But wait a minute. These men were Jews! Well, yes, but unbelieving Jews, you add. No, they were praying Jews. They lifted their voices in prayer to God, believing that He could heal them. "Jesus, Master, have mercy upon us," they cried out. They lifted their voices loudly. "Jesus, Master, have mercy upon us."

They were men of prayer. But they were not men of praise. Like so many others who pray for mercy— like me and like you—when the mercy came, the prayer of praise did not come. Like so many others, they prayed, but when the prayers were answered, they forgot to be grateful.

I feel that there are many among us who are the same. We may be devoted to our time of prayer. Every morning and every night and throughout the day we spend much time in prayer. We may be praying men and women. We may have many petitions, long lists of supplications, yet praise is seldom heard from our lips. Like the lepers, we can be men of prayer, and men of belief, and men of obedience; but yet not be men of praise.

The sin the lepers committed was not one of disbelief, for they believed with all their hearts that Jesus could heal them. It was not one of disobedience, for they followed His command to go show themselves to the priests. They did not hesitate, they did not procrastinate, they did not rationalize. No, they had too much at stake to do that. They went as they were told. But when the answer to their prayer came, they did not praise the Source of that answer. They were not men of praise.

We can pray . . . and believe . . . and obey . . . and still displease God. For we can pray and grumble, believe and grumble, and obey and grumble. We can do them all with the thought in our hearts, "Yes, God, but it's a raw deal." We can still be thankless and still focus our minds on those things which we don't have but wish we did. We can, in short, be ungrateful.

Why? Because too many of us, even as Christians, have a "fly complex." Do you know what that is? You have a fly complex when a fly falls in your ointment and you can no longer see the ointment for the fly. Instead of being thankful for the ointment, all you do is count fly's legs.

Yes, Christians with a fly complex cannot see the good or be thankful for it. They see only what is wrong with everything and the faults in everybody. Therefore, they are not thankful for anything or anybody. "Neither were (they) thankful. . . . For this cause God gave them up . . ." (Rom. 1:21,26).

Where does the word "thank" come from? It comes from the same root as the word "think". Many people do not thank because they do not think. There is a hymn that says, "Trust and obey, for there's no other way to be happy in Jesus, but to trust and obey." Notice that it doesn't say, "Trust and obey, for there's no other way to be saved." We are not saved by trusting *and* obeying but by trusting only.

But once we are in Jesus we must trust and obey. I am sure that there are many people who trust and obey and still are not happy in Jesus because we haven't learned to praise. There is another hymn which tells us to "count your many blessings . . . and it will surprise you what the Lord has done." Yes, if we do that, we will be surprised at what God has actually done for us.

The Bible says, "In every thing give thanks" (1 Thess. 5:18); "Giving thanks always for all things unto God and the Father in the name of our Lord Jesus Christ" (Eph. 5:20). It is not only possible for the Christian to be "giving thanks always for all things unto God," it is absolutely necessary if he is to know happiness and blessing as a Christian. As William Law, an eighteenth century English clergyman declared, "If anyone could tell you the shortest, surest way to all happiness and perfection, he must tell you to make it a rule to yourself to thank and praise God for everything that happens to you. For it is certain that whatever seeming calamity happens to you, if you thank and praise God for it, you turn it into a blessing. . . ."

Nowhere is the principle that "giving thanks always for all things unto God" results in blessing better illustrated than in an incident narrated by Corrie ten Boom in her book, *The Hiding Place* written with John and Elizabeth Sherrill. Corrie and her sister, Betsie, two Dutch spinster sisters, were put in prison by the Nazis during World War II for hiding Jews in their house in Amsterdam.

In one of the prison camps where they were confined, conditions were so bad that their quarters were infested with fleas. Betsie, the older of the two sisters and a continually Spirit-filled woman, wanted to give thanks to God even for the fleas. The young Corrie could not understand how one could be thankful for such a thing as a flea, but she followed her sister's lead and did praise God for them.

Later they discovered that the comparative freedom the women enjoyed in their barracks, the freedom which allowed them to share the gospel with so many other prisoners, was due to the fact that the guards would not enter the flea-ridden room! God had used even the fleas to His glory . . . and the sisters were thankful!

Thanksgiving transforms the human personality. Perhaps the greatest gift you could give your wives, men, would be to learn how to be thankful instead of grumbling. You can't grumble in gratitude, you know. Maybe the greatest gift you can give your husbands, wives, would be to learn to be grateful instead of complaining.

I wonder if we look upon complaining as the sin that it really is, the sin of ingratitude. It's like saying, "God, you've got it all fouled up down here. God, you don't know what you're doing. God, I'm not thankful with what you've done with my life." Complaining is, in fact, a form of rebellion against the throne of heaven. And it has its negative effect upon our personalities just as surely as do the diseases and ills that decay our physical bodies.

"Well," you may say, "thanksgiving may focus my attention on the things that are good and take it away from the things that are bad. And I can see that this is a good idea psychologically." But it is more than that. It is good to forget what is bad and look at the things that are good, counting your blessings as you go. But that's not all there is to thanksgiving and praise.

It also is realizing that God has promised to work all things together for good for those who love Him. That He will turn everything that comes into the lives of Christians to good. Don't misunderstand what I am saying. The Bible doesn't teach that everything works out all right for everybody in the end. In fact, Scripture teaches that everything works out miserably for most people in the end. It teaches that most people live a pretty meaningless life, die without Christ and go to hell forever. "Enter ye in at the strait gate: for wide is the gate, and broad is the way, that leadeth to destruction, and many there be which go in thereat: because strait is the gate, and narrow is the way, which leadeth unto life, and few there be that find it" (Matt. 7:13,14).

But for those who are God's people, there is this promise: "And we know that all things work together for good to them that love God, to them who are the called according to his purpose" (Rom. 8:28). This is God's absolute guarantee to His people that no matter what comes into their lives, He will by the amazing alchemy of His grace work it eventually to their good. There's no exception!

Therefore, we can "give thanks always for all things unto God" (Eph. 5:20), as the Bible commands us to do. "In every thing give thanks" (1 Thess. 5:18). Everything! Whatever it is, we can thank God—and we should—if we are His children.

Have you seen answers to prayer recently? Praise Him! Have you felt His working in your life? Praise Him! Have you grown as a believer? Praise Him! Have you discovered the love of studying and reading His Word? Praise Him! Is there some misfortune that has befallen you or your family? Praise Him—by faith—even though the last thing on earth you may feel like doing is being grateful for the calamity or tragedy.

Since you're going to be praising Him for all eternity, you might as well start now!

Putting It All Together 7

God talks with me. I talk with God. Put it all together, and it spells dialogue. The Christian's dialogue with God. That's what this book is all about, and that's what we've been talking about from the very first chapter.

God Talks with Me

First we learned that the Bible is the inspired Word of God, God's love letter to all mankind. Then we discussed prophecy and how the infallible fulfillment of prophetic utterances gives credence to the Scripture's truthfulness and inspiration. The biblical mark of a prophet is that his prophecy always comes true and is never wrong.

God has never failed to work out that which He has prophesied. And you can bet that He never will in the future! We studied some of the prophecies about Jesus Christ which prove that He was—and is—the Messiah talked about in the Old Testament. In short, we learned a little about the Bible's claim to be divine revelation.

What an exciting fact this is! Man has at his disposal the very words, thoughts, and past actions of God! If you are a history buff, you know how exciting it is to uncover a book that reveals to you a culture you are particularly interested in. Archaeologists' discoveries about certain civilizations are fascinating because these discoveries give us more light about them, thus making them more interesting to us. And here in the Bible we have the whole panorama of mankind in one book—all man's failures, his successes, his wartime forays, his peaceful endeavors—all told in the light of his relationship to the God who created him.

For the believer in Jesus Christ the Bible is much, much more than just a history of mankind. It is God's manifesto on daily living, on heaven, on judgment, on righteousness, in short, on all the important issues of life. God is telling us not only how life was thousands of years ago, but how life should be lived today—by you and by me. So in the second chapter of this book we learned how to study God's Word in order to get the most out of it both spiritually and practically. The Bible is not absorbed into one's system like air. It must be digested in daily doses. It must be studied through, prayed over, reflected upon and shared out. Knowing how to do these things with the Bible can mean the difference between a spiritually mature believer and one who never grows beyond his salvation experience.

I Talk with God

If the Bible is God's way of speaking to man, prayer is man's way of speaking to God. In the other chapters of this book we learned much about prayer, what it is, how to do it, when it will work . . . and when it won't and why. We studied prayer in relationship to the rest of the armor of God. And above all, we discussed the importance of prayer in the believer's life.

If two people are going to get to know one another, there must be communication both ways. There must be dialogue. It is not enough that one person do all the talking and the other all the listening. And so it is with our relationship with God. As He speaks to us, we must learn to speak also to Him about the deepest things of our heart and mind in order that He may become closer and more real to us day by day. And as we share our lives with Him through the utterances of prayer, we grow in the Lord and our knowledge of Him.

Then we talked about the promises of God and what they can mean in our lives. Like blank checks made out to us and waiting to be cashed, these promises can mean the difference between an exciting, supernatural life and one that is dull and mundane. We learned what some of these promises of God in His Word are so that we can take advantage of them by claiming them and cashing them in.

Finally, we discussed the important aspect of praising God. When an answer to prayer comes, when a blessing comes our way, when God has done something that is beyond our comprehension, when we merely want to show our awe of Him, we should praise Him. And we learned that even when things don't seem to be going according to our own plans, we should still praise Him. Why? Because one of the great promises in the Bible is that God is working all things together for good to those who are His children. Even though we can't see the good in a given situation, we can thank Him through faith in that promise.

Putting It Together

You now have the basics for growing in faith in Jesus Christ. You know a little more about studying the Bible and about praying. With these weapons in hand, you can conquer anything. Anything! You need be afraid of nothing. And as you begin to use these weapons, you will find yourself growing in Christ. Others will see Him in you and will be drawn to Him. Your whole outlook on life will change. Relationships with people will become sweeter and more meaningful. Your job will not be such a burden. Doing for others will be a great joy. In short, you will become more and more like your Saviour.

Taking It from Here

But don't stop with this book! Study and learn more! Digest other books on prayer and Bible study. Talk to people about what they have learned in their readings. Share with your fellow believers the great revelations you have had from God. Always be growing and searching and willing to learn.

That is my prayer for you in Jesus, that establishing this dialogue with God will be only the beginning of a glorious relationship with Him that will bear more and more fruit in the months and years to come. That's really what the Christian life is all about: bearing fruit for God's Glory.

The fruit of Christ's perfection in the believer can spread around the world as thousands of Christians become more intimate with their Creator. But it begins with you and with your own private Bible study and prayer time. May God richly bless you as He talks with you, and you talk with Him. And out of this continuing dialogue may you live for Him more and more effectively each day.